You There, Reading This Poem

You There, Reading This Poem

R. Steve Martin

You There, Reading This Poem

ISBN: 979-8-89933-020-9 (Paperback)
Library of Congress Control Number: 2026904630

Cover/Book Design: Erin Mann
Interior Layout: Seed Bed Ted

Printed in the United States of America
First printing 2026

Redhawk Publications
The Catawba Valley Community College Press
2550 US Hwy 70 SE
Hickory, NC 28602
https://redhawkpublications.com

Dedication

As a garden noiselessly goes about
loving me and loving me
I hear the sounds

Table of Contents

Writing

Love

Transition

Becoming

Writing

On a wisp of wire

This poem
is walking a tightrope
between peace and affirmation
and this poem loves words
unsteady words
unpredictable words
words that will throw you down a well
or pick you up for a ride to heaven
it's a thrill-seeking kind of poem
and it won't hesitate to juggle
clubs ladders pets spin pies
and for the first time
and without further ado
this poem will use a wheelbarrow
and needs some passengers.

The journey of words

My wife's a professional editor
a trained killer
of mistakes
of the written word
and she loves it
and she loves me
and I love to write words
and I love her
and after I've written
a lot of words
I say Hon
you read my stuff
and it's like
a Quentin Tarantino movie
with words
words that are weak
and untested and proud
who go through hell
to find out who they are

A bard rides poetry for winning time and form

With chaps
left hand on reins
right hand ninety degrees taut and up
climb a bull named Sleepy
spin digging out the gate—Hee ahh
jump in midair like on a griddle
head turns counterclockwise
end twist clockwise
whirl bounce slip
flung hard to the ground hit running
from Sleepy's quick stomping turn
God bless the clowns
head bent
bruised
dust hat on leg
no qualifying time
no cigar
just more bull

Things

I feel guilty about all the things I have,
like my things will somehow make me feel,
good about myself,
how you look at me,
want what I got,
I want what you got,
but like an opiate this feeling
of being loved
because I have things
amazing things,
beautiful things,
wears off,
and I need pumping up all over again,
and it doesn't stop with just things,
I have been eyeing your poetry
for quite some time.

I wish I had written it.

Wife finding time to write

She gets up
a thief
before work, or after work,
before bed, or after bed,
while in bed
anytime
she is not in the driver's seat
of cooking, or working,
or in the pursuit of
what we do to make a living
before it becomes later,
before the parade has passed,
and the confetti is thrown,
and life has set its agenda,
she finds the time
between appointments already made,
between the things that must be done,
like the next holiday,
she waits patiently for it to become
my turn to drive, and squints into the sun
struggling through the glare of her laptop

punches in one more word,
one more thought
in her
no holds barred assault
to reveal herself
painting
with her
heart,
and mind,
and soul—
this is who I am,
this is how I dream,
because the currency
of this world is time,
so she steals

The Alps of Anson County

I'm a terrible thief she said
as she caught me hunched over my laptop
secretively pounding at the keys
where does she get this stuff
my wife just compared the biggest hill in our
    hometown
East Wade
to the Sochi 22nd Winter Olympic Game ski
    jumpers
really, she said
I bet it is no bigger than what we use to sled on
to which I blinked
so she tucked in her chin
and pointing with her forehead
said a bit stronger "really"
and for emphasis paused
and that's when my head exploded
I could see myself on that hill
my sled bent
my cotton gloves
my two pairs of socks

brogans long johns
and everybody and everything
is wet and cold and laughing
under the weight of children
stacked precariously as peas
careening off the Alps of Anson County
the mountainside of the world

Sign up at Poetry Night

Many poets had arrived early
looked over the signup sheet and had already added their
    names
but not for slot number one and number two
what sorcery is this I thought in the briefest of moments
as I scrawled my name beside number one and sat down
I started to feel like the first guy who ate a tomato
the tomato
part of the nightshade family included toxic plants
and the other poets knew this
and I just ate one
I stood up and filled my slot with words
I prayed the words would become a poem
I prayed they'd see the inner workings of a fellow traveler
struggling beside them
hammering away
mining my emotions that bubbled into thoughts
represented by my words
words carefully chosen
and parceled and distilled
into an emotional photograph

of my journey with them
as we hurl together on this ball of clay
as they all watch to see
if I had been poisoned by a tomato

I'm very sorry I didn't have supper ready

I'm very sorry I didn't have supper ready
when you came home late
and I'd been here all day
playing
mostly writing
I did clean up today though
tidied
took care of kitty
took out the garbage
vacuumed
made some soup
because I felt awful
after I saw
how disappointed you were
enough to start writing again.

Raising the alphabet

I've had it
today
I will start minding
just my Ps and Qs
and let the rest of the alphabet
individuate
without any prodding
or direction or guidance
or well-intentioned bossy
behavior on my part
whatsoever
I will not tell the alphabet
who it is
anymore
so
the letters can decide
for themselves
what makes them different
from the other letters
because
thay kneed two fide ouwt foar temselzes
who thay R.

Poetry, and nature

It was early
about five
when I started to dust off my metaphors
the moon that lights my path is my friend
except when crescent
it's not a very good friend
clearly, I was struggling
when in the corner of the living room
I noticed a bat hanging from the ceiling
a little brown bat about the size of my hand
to which I took umbrage
for nature cannot just
insert itself into a poem
without invitation
it's not proper
then I thought my God
there's a bat in the house
asleep
and I had been writing awhile
and that I murmur loudly when I write
I hope I didn't wake it up

murmuring helps me feel the sounds of words
before they are born and go through their
    seasons
they live out their summers
full of joy and sorrow and adventure
then the furnace popped on
and I remembered winter is coming
it must be cold outside
poor fellow
he is kind of cute
and what should I call him
when company comes for tea
Shadow nope
Baltazar nope
Vlad nope
Fred is nice

One of the things that stops me from writing poetry

One of the things that stops me from writing
poetry is
the thought
it must be good
but once I accept the poem
as bad-tempered
a scoundrel
with a penchant
for cliches
run on sentences
refusing to face
an honest thought
then the sky's the limit
sometimes the thing just wanders
about the page like a scout from an ant colony
leaving a scent as it looks for a crumb
but if it loses its way
and loops back on itself
the poem will walk in circles for days
but sometimes

after being exhausted
the poem finds itself
and makes connections
that are dusty and lost and frightening
and it wants to share what it found inside itself
that looks very similar to what it sees in you

A smoky little poem

I love a smoky little poem
in a long khaki skirt
with 5th Avenue hips
that
go
all
the
way
down
the
cat
walk
with little slits that go
right up the sides
and stop just short
of where they should
and your eyes,
keep
going
on
down
the
page.

Here's to another rough draft

To all the poems
who drink
and stay up late
gap toothed
and handsome
and proud
and spill onto the page
old and bald and fat
and cry into their beer
and we feel sorry for them
and rub their heads
and say all the right things
for a poem in this condition

here's to another rough draft

I was in love with my words

I was in love with my words,
where they were lissome and light,
thin-wristed, and slender-tongued,
I quarreled barrel-chested
into the night
troubled and hardly stood,
they moved high heeled,
and lipstick gorgeous,
and I, I was bowlegged
with dirt under my nails
and brown shoes,
my words were sonnets,
and the sonnets were flowers,
and the metaphors became songs,
and when my words loved,
I sighed back at them,
they were moonlit, and candle
and I was torch on a stick,
I was soup spoon,
and they were Paris at night
young, and in love,

they were silken grace,
and when they moved,
I could only dream
clinging claw-fisted,
and needy,
I was Quasimodo,
and my words
were Esmeralda.

If you go anywhere else to read a poem you'll pay too much

We've got more metaphors than sense

and similes like none you've seen

onomatopoeia bam

got you covered

hyperbole check

best poem ever

alliterations

dance on down

and we're not done yet

two personifications for the price of one

this poem wants your business

this poem is crazy

and don't wait too long

because we're selling poetic devices

like biscuits on gravy

we're the last adorable kitten

your dying mother will ever have

we will not be under emoted

we're dealing.

Love

Walk at first light

My wife and I take
our walk at first light
to the park play Pokémon
on our cell phones
and I cling to the warmth
of who she is to me
hold hands
as we cross streets
and intersections
and occasionally
we stop
and fight battles
as two children at play
we have mellowed
into the sweetest couple
experiencing this world
more fully
with each step we take
the insects wake up first
then the birds
and as we listen

across the sky
the sun stirs
in streaks of pastel bands
described by Homer
and we linger there

Potatoes and me

Growing up on the mill village
we had only the essentials but by God
we had a deep fryer and a potato press
we weren't savages
I love fried potatoes
scalloped with cheese
boiled
mashed with butter stirred in a pot
or covered in olive oil
baked in the oven
till the skin splits
with chunks of butter
not yet melted
just the other day my wife introduced me to
    gnocchi
and I thought hello gnocchi
where have you been all my life
there is this family lore that once
I cooked three kinds of potatoes for supper
mashed fried and boiled
mistakes have been made

I have no defense
a few years ago my son altered my Netflix
    profile name to read
"Mashed Potatoes"
I haven't bothered to change it
so on Valentine's Day
knowing my wife would understand
the depth of my love
I looked straight into her eyes and said,
"I love you more than potatoes"
and she said,
"it's not nice to lie"
and that's when I looked at my feet.

Night out with Wine Woman

Meeting once a month the women of the
neighborhood gather
and occasionally men are invited at the whim of
the host
so, I found myself at this old home wrapped in
porches
overlooking the town as the sun set on the
mountains
on my third plate of cheesecake crackers chicken
salad
pecan crusted sugary whatchamacallits and a
deviled egg
and each time I sat down from the snack table
I raved unapologetically about how wonderful
the deviled eggs were
found myself in the presence of the owner of the
deviled eggs
a culinary Buddha and my wife
recognizing an expert started asking questions
how do you get the eggshell off
I'm always tearing my eggs apart

and Buddha spoke
I bring the eggs to room temperature
a pot of water to boil with a lot of salt
slide the eggs into the water
boil fifteen minutes
ice bath peel then be amazed
and we sat around listening
like it was the last will and testament
of a dying rich uncle
and the secret to her deviled eggs
vinegar and my wife
a culinary Buddha in her own right added
I like a little curry powder in my deviled eggs
and the master
acknowledging a clever twist when she heard
    one said,
sexy
those are sexy eggs

and everybody agreed

The recipe

Take some salmon filets olive oil
a sprig of rosemary and pepper heavily
broil ten minutes to each side
then rub raw garlic in a bowl
tossing the hearts of Romaine lettuce
mixed with oil and red wine vinegar
grate some sharp cheddar and parmesan
over the top
with strawberries on the side
I use two or three
now with more garlic and oil
broil the bread till brown
light a candle
pour a glass of wine
I prefer red a couple of years in the making
flowers cut from the yard doesn't matter what
  type
some music R & B opera blues rock
not too loud
that you would notice
and arrange what you have on a table

greet her as she comes home tired from work
and place your hands around her head
like you are holding something tender
kiss the top of her crown
then count to yourself — one two three
she's yours.

This life—hers, mine, ours

At work her purpose is
to transform what is good
into what is better
she is a tour de force
and personal baggage is
cordoned off
by professional courtesy of purpose
but at home
we are our loving selves
our tired selves
our selves that need nourishment
our becoming restored whole selves
so we can go back out into this world selves
we are spirits of charity and love
and support to the other
through the many places
we have followed each other
sometimes my job and sometimes
I followed you to yours
and now over the ages
I say over the ages because

we have been together
a long time in this field of play
and give and take and pull
and tug and sometimes
I forget who we are
to the other
so when I say Dearheart
could you drain the noodles
a bit more
the spaghetti sauce is watery
and this upsets you
I mean to say
you are such a wonderful cook
my life has been so much more
because you are in it
you pave my steps with flowers
forever turning down my covers
when I am tired
so many people depend on you
you are such a good person
God help me but I do love
the perfect way you forget
to drain the noodles

The bulls of Pamplona

One day my teenage children and I
were around the supper table,
Luke may have said it first,
maybe Mary
I don't remember,
but shut up was said,
and my wife does not allow
our children to say shut up.
shut up is so Neanderthal, brusque, uncivil,
and not a way to interact with one's fellow
travelers
of this life,
she is very firm on this,
and I agree,
but tonight
she was out of town on business
when the first volleys of shut up were fired,
and one was not getting much of a grip
on the other,
so undisturbed it went,
I could feel the air waiting for my adult

intervention,
and I remember how we were laughing,
and how much we loved each other
in that moment of no rules,
so I said
both of you shut up,
and it was the running of the bulls
down the streets of Pamplona—
I turned them loose.

Close to my daughter's due date

Cape Canaveral Mission Control called saying
she was two centimeters dilated, and
fifty percent effaced,
but it was not until my wife heard that the
    midwife said,
she could feel the plates on the top of the baby's
    head,
that she went cracker dog
packing for her upcoming trip to Texas
I came upon her in the bedroom
with a backpack stuffed with her things strapped
    to her back,
about forty pounds or so jostling the weight,
shifting it around to test the comfort of the
    straps,
like she was going to tote this satchel of bricks
    across purgatory,
and the Houston and Austin airports, and hell
    itself
to get to this birthing, no problem,
I talked her into putting it into a checked suitcase

with the laptop as a carry on,
sweetness, and spice is what they are,
until the real work starts,
God knew what he was doing
when he gave women this job,
I feel the same anticipation,
the same excitement
as when Neil Armstrong
stepped out onto the moon,
one small step for man,
one giant leap for Grandpa

Babysitting grandson for daughter and husband out on the town

Entropy is asleep upstairs,
and the magazines are less some pages,
the corners bent
covers ripped off
have been picked up
and folded back beside the couch,
but they are frightened,
the stackable bowls,
the wind-up thingies,
the mélange of toys, bits of paper
whatever has not been randomized
strewn shredded pounded turned sucked on bit,
the toddler bowls with the little suction feet
specially made to brace themselves
against blustery dining conditions
fought the hardest,
but ended up on the floor anyway
with the rest of the house,
and the Little Tikes lawn mower that goes—
pop pop pop when it comes through,

and pop pop pop when it goes back
mowed over what is left
it is as if a hurricane came through,
and they retired its name out of respect

My son and I attend a zombie movie

It's surprising
how the principles of zombie dynamics keep
    changing
you spot a zombie
ribs showing groaning
masquerading as slow and stupid
and it spots you
and comes running like a coffee lover after
    espresso
welcome to your new life—
zombies that run
but in this movie
they get smart
so my son and I,
eating popcorn, and a box
of sprinkled-covered chocolate stars,
wonder what will happen next,
because the zombies,
they got business to do,
and my son and I,
we got father son stuff to take care of.

He was in kindergarten, and I was on car duty

There were only a few kids left
as I sat on a bench
and even then
he had to look up
as if taking in the full height of a redwood
but he had to ask
"Mr. Martin, where's your mama?"
and I couldn't tell
if he was curious
or if he was concerned
because it was late
and his mama was on her way
where was mine?
where was my anchor
from which to explore this world
unconditionally reassured,
he was ten feet tall
and stood on a rock.

The sweetness and ridiculous nature of us

This fight started when I asked my wife
if she had ever heard of
what kind of sound a rhino makes
and showed her a video
and her focus became oh,
that's not a real rhino sound
because it's a baby rhino
and my side
the side of reason
I said it doesn't matter
and to chase this rabbit
farther on down the road came
oh, they're not even African rhinos
they're Asian rhinos
implying
they don't make
the same kinds of sounds
the dangerous bloodthirsty
full-grown African rhino
everybody really wants to hear makes
and nobody wants to hear this

because this video is crap
and my taste in finding
entertaining useless videos is crap
and I am crap and everything's crap
wounded she had me cornered
so I counter-retorted
they're just rhinos
who cares if they're grown
or Asian or African
and then delivering the
solid wallop to her glass jaw
I said
you never enjoy anything
which I admit
never
may have been
a poor choice of words
to which I regret saying
to which she asked me to take back
and I wouldn't
so she didn't kiss me
when she went to bed
and I slept on the couch

and in the morning
she wanted to kiss me
and I said no
and crossed my arms
like I had a force field around me
so she just leaned over
and kissed me twice
on the top of the head
and that's when I knew
I didn't

It started with a sore throat

It started with a sore throat
that went on for weeks
then the flu
a dry hacking of this life
there was nothing extraneous
left over about me
I felt as if I would
never recover
never go back to work
never return to what I was
I had given up
I forgot who I used to be
so I watched World War II movies
one after the other
fought in Europe
fought in the South Pacific
fought Guadalcanal twice
the Warsaw ghetto
I was right there
shivering and shaking
in my underwear and my wife

Mother Teresa
my goddess nonpareil
bought some mineral oil
and camphor and menthol
and eucalyptus and lavender
and poured it all into a bowl
of boiling water and with a towel
draped over my head
I breathed it all in—
this life I have
and I remembered.

Le snuggerie

Okay, I accept your taunt,
let's compare your nest with my nest,
by the sofa where I read, write,
watch videos, eat, drink, nap,
I have a pair of shoes, days of socks,
poems printed, reposed, and coiled about the
    floor,
books sleeping, a blanket trying to crawl off the
    sofa,
remotes, a wicker basket for trash,
and the basket is not an exact place,
a point of longitude, and latitude,
it is an approximation, a province, a region,
not unlike one of France, Champagne maybe,
distinguished by its cooler climate,
or the wetter Bordeaux with its
    beautiful winding rivers,
and life-affirming moisture, moisture that defines
the very nature of its grape,
and you my dear with your laptop and teacups,
sundry glasses, and books, and blankets

sprawled, and strewn about
make our nine-foot sectional sofa look
pinched.
but dearheart, pumpkins, true love
you are the buttery Chardonnay
to my crisp Chablis
the contents of our life cannot be penned,
but spills out onto the floral wooded hillsides
    of our living room,
our cathedral,
of our retreat,
our study,
mon amour—
our snuggerie.

My wife away on a trip

You were not here
so I took your tea
the Earl Grey
the Chinese Fortune
the chai spice
the blended teas
of ginger, cinnamon, and clove
the Chinese oolong
and the black teas
crisp, complicated, girly teas,
that were waiting in the pantry
and the tools for making
the honey pot with the little wooden
dowel, so you
that was waiting. And
the little finger bowls
that huddled around the teapot
like lost children
the African violet
over the sink
in need of care

and my tea bag
at the bottom of my cup,
and I,
and the water
waiting to boil
because you were not here.

A big part of my day is messing with Julie

It's an art that requires some finesse
like jostling the car with no overt turns or jerks
while driving as natural as possible
as she applies lipstick is one
the first week we were married
I stood outside her shower silently stabbing
at the curtain with a banana while she screamed
forty-two years later I learned
thoughtfully prepared meals loading the
    dishwasher
dividing up chores a kiss on the forehead
saying I'm sorry and I love you
often and daily is her preferred love language
I know this because
I have put in years of trial and error
to find out what works
poetry is a helper
sometimes
I tell her what I'm thinking and she listens
and sometimes I listen and sometimes
she likes for me to listen without trying to solve
    her problems

doing things we love together helps
singing
long talks with coffee
with a yellow silk scarf rolled around her head
and her thick brown bed hair raging rebellious
    and defiant
and as we do chores around the house
we throw kisses and taunts and jabs
like professional boxers at play
in one continuous affirmation
we move through our lives
and when our children
and their children and spouses visit
our world dances
and the house becomes
a flower in bloom
and before we sleep
before her hair tangles again
she likes to snuggle on one side
and we hold each other
and just as sleep approaches
and it is not possible to catch another moment
we turn over

Close to you

There has always been this unspoken struggle in
    our house
chores are divided up into floors and cooking
    and dishes and laundry
but I control the remote and buy what I want when I want it
and go about demanding plates of pepper bacon
    for breakfast
with eggs over light and sunflower bread toast
and she goes off to work leaving a sprig of
    flowers on the side
but the true powers are in those hips
she swings around like shotgun shells
I follow her around places stores walks and
    sometimes
I leave the door open when I go to bed early
just to hear her move around the living room
    when I sleep
when she writes a school paper I talk too much
and she tells me to stop
I do stop but walk in now and then to check
just in case she changes her mind

or finds a point to take a break
and sometimes I say hell this is just too good to
  keep to myself
and say can I tell you something
and she pretends to be exasperated says what
and I say I just read on the internet that in this
  study
they found that the smell of grapefruit makes
  women seem
six years younger and she says that's the last
  time
and I walk off sheepishly till I come in on her again
when she takes a trip I ask her if she has checked
  her tires
and of course no give her car full service
car maintenance and yard maintenance
seem to make her feel kept
we drive off and do the relative thing
or the beach thing or the restaurant thing
and come back home each to their own space
all the time nudging each other
till we say come on in

Dear love

When the litter box you carried fell apart
and released its entire malodorous contents
onto our carpeted stairs and down the hall
coming to a rest under the little table
where we keep our keys
I'm very sorry I laughed
forgive me
it's just
I've never been
gleeful
and horrified
it may have appeared
I was laughing at you
that I was insensitive
reveling in your misfortune
what I meant to say was
I am sorry
this is so unfortunate
let me help you
it could have happened
to anybody

just leave it now
I'll take care of you
I am wounded
and the whole world is wounded
go lie down with a cup of cocoa

I never could dance

I never could dance,
it's a mental thing really,
a cage
I have placed myself into,
a box
like the one that contains
kitchen matches,
always keep matches in the box,
if loosely scattered about,
some unknown surface,
cat fur maybe, might ignite it,
and there goes the house, I have
given up thinking I might change,
I do love dancing with you,
in secret, it makes me blush,
but oh how I have courted you,
with my cowboy hat, spurs,
and boots, I grin with you
in my arms using my words,
my words are carrying
a rose between their teeth

I hear the sounds

You clean my socks
have my children
if wheat needs a harvest
you are the combine that rolls over the fields
the blade that receives the crop
the oven split loaves
you are the table set before me
the smells of winter storms
and the stillness of fall's
rose-colored canopy of leaves
I step in quiet step
I see the sounds of footsteps
when scattered about a garden
my soul moves and bends
my love is as a hush
and I bow
and on my knees
hear your petals' deafening sound
as a garden noiselessly goes about
loving me and loving me
I hear the sounds.

Why the stars sent the moon a dozen roses

Sometimes things go horribly wrong
the stars had crossed the moon
when the moon
hadn't bothered anybody
just minding her own business
watching English garden
detective murder mysteries
the mother lode of girly escapes
gardens and mysteries
when out the blue the stars
for no reason
the stars
lash out at the moon
and planetary bodies cross
and the moon goes crescent
and going to work the next day
with the moon right there
in the front seat
beside the stars
the stars had to wear a wool coat
things got so chilly

the moon just sat there
looked straight ahead
wouldn't say a word
the stars felt bad
because the stars can't shine
without the moon
without the moon
the stars have no reason
to be in the sky
the stars come out at night
just to be
with the moon
so to uncross things
to keep day from turning
into starless night
and at a time
when everybody
would see and know
how amazing and wonderful
the moon really is
how much she is needed
and loved and appreciated
a dozen roses is sent to the moon's day job.

A wonderful life

There is always a moment
when I recover from an all-consuming illness
like the flu
when I realize I am no longer sick
and what is important comes into focus
all the things I had forgotten
that I had taken for granted
how unique my contributions are
how dependent I am on everyone who loves me
and how dependent they are on me
and even the people I don't know whose lives
    I've changed
"It's a Wonderful Life" sort of moment
I am Jimmy Stewart
returning to this world
fumbling with that loose knob
coming off the stair railing
where I stop
and kiss it

Transition

The therapist

As a heated wool blanket
thrown over my inward world
daring it to peek out
from its secret storm of tears
with a nod, a smile, a what's that
a touch on the shoulder
of lessons on how men embrace
and how it feels
to be with someone
in that moment
holding
the other up
reveling in who they are
whispering as God might echo in a canyon
no one believes in you more than me
and listening so intent that breath becomes
    shallow
and takes moments
and forgets and stops
for fear you might miss a pause a moment a nod
so hangs every word

as wind that sits among the leaves
and waits for permission to move
and then moves as one heart
I know you
and that parts of me
are somehow
like parts of you
and that my story
is somehow
your story
a sacred story
a sacred time
a sacred journey
of which you held to a light
and what I was hiding
somehow grew
as something with tap roots
and I took that first breath greedily in the sun
and you were there to receive me

Stormy

The bobcat comes
on little stormy feet.
It prowls looking
over mountains and woods
on paws without a peep.
And then moves on
little stormy feet.

With thanks to Carl Sandburg

In this picture

In this picture of my mother, and brothers,
and me,
my father's presence is there only as one
who holds the camera,
and as I look at this moment
it is as if I am seeing through his eyes,
Mother holding my shoulder
to keep me from tumbling off the mountain,
and she is so fresh, and crisp, and new,
and we are all puppies around her,
and it is documented like the great history we
are,
like kings and queens we are standing,
our grins unfurling
as we pose in front of an old Ford
with its fat, white-walled tires,
this iconic moment
in black and white
of our family
on vacation,
a snowflake
frozen
in the hands
of a camera

Up since 2 a.m.

Up since 2 a.m.
now—11 a.m.
the mama and daddy—spent.
Baby—born.
Grandma baby video—
taken, emailed, posted.
World—informed.
He lies in a bassinet in the corner,
wide awake,
swaddled,
tucked in
with an oversized toboggan cap
taking in the room
with just his eyes
not saying,
what he is looking at,
just trying
to figure out,
what he got into.

Start over

I will now and then play
the video clip
of our grandchildren I made
the last time
they were in town
both in diapers
the older one would
chew a piece of paper up
like a dog and the younger one
would laugh and laugh
at his brother snarling
as he tore into the paper
as snips and pieces
fell to the floor
the smaller grandson
would laugh in delight
laugh from his gut
laugh like the world
was a flower
that had just said boo
and always my wife

would hear and smile

and come over beside me

and say

make it bigger

start over.

My daughter sings

She is but, one step away
from the sand pile singing.
The one where
the front wheel is broken
and the axle,
the one that keeps repeating itself,
and gets louder with each broken verse:
the "Little Red Wagon" song.
I can see her head tilt,
determined to get even larger,
from where she was,
to where she will be,
and with each repetition,
the Tonka truck shovel,
the flying sand,
the hair in braids,
sing-songy, and locomotive,
I see my daughter—
white sand in a box,
marked off for play,
and the two by sixes

I picked from a lumber yard,
from not so, busy a time, when
the unexpected, the unnoted,
would pause, and take a breath,
I can hear her getting louder,
and put my coffee and paper down,
I never like to stir the cream,
but let it swirl
into something Colombian
like the slope of a forest,
some burlap, a burro,
one carrying a too large load
about town,
over a mountain,
and I listened
to my daughter singing,
her lungs struggling,
the very air expanding
to keep up,
and I know it will not be long,
till the wheels fall off.

I write this to my daughter

I left a little girl for the first time
at her college dorm with things unsaid
and as I drove off knew
the parting was unfinished
for our hearts had announced it
twisting me inside
and my tears spoke the mystery
of things sacred
and I felt like something was being torn
crudely abruptly off my very soul
and that something tugged at my fabric
and that fabric wanted things to be the same
and yearned in a role
that has remained all these years
for I must keep you safe
and I must keep you close
I must teach you the ways
I remember your first step
as a toddler as you shakily held
to furniture to cross a room
and I am proud and exhilarated

and frightened all at the same time
for nothing could cut my heart
as harm that comes your way
so I am vigilant and careful
and as you grow watch imperceptibly
as my role changes and I marvel
at what you have become
so beautiful so beautiful
and what happened
happened in its own time
and would not wait
but marched as water or wind
moves over rock
and somehow even the rock
could not be as before
and I a not-so-perfect father
thought there was time for practice
time to become and stop and say
this is my daughter
the person I am so proud of
who I love so much
and there is not one thing she can do
that would make me love her more

nor is there one thing she can do
that would make me love her less
and she would know this
because I would say it often
as you were passing in my life
but it all comes
unannounced quickly
and I did not notice
your time with us
had passed
without the proper words
to reveal my heart
not just in this moment
but in all the moments
I have not said enough
what a joy you have been
and too much I have said
what was done
was not as
I would have done
and I never told you
how precious you are
so I say those things now

what I have left unsaid
so that you will know with my words
what my heart has always been
and how it is I
who has had the privilege
to know you as a child

so parting that night unfinished
you ride your bike to our hotel
limp
the rain kisses your scattered spirit
and leaves a trail of gossamer fabric
that collects at our door
your mother and I
we kiss you and set you free.

Tired

I lay in bed, unshaven
dreaming I had quit my job,
I no longer wanted to do
the things I had done—
the mortgage,
the car,
not one more decision
I can't even decide
what bread to buy
at the grocery store—
sliced, unsliced, wheat
which batteries last
longer, cheaper, better,
they place them at the checkout counter
where I am the weakest,
after all the decisions I have made
that have yet to make me happy,
and when I go home,
even the cat rubs up against me
making demands,
I will not do it.
I refuse to pull her tail one more time.

A picture of exhaustion

My wife
asleep on the couch
crumpled from the week
under the weight of
petals of blankets
with her one arm dangling out
she is trying to remember
how liberty used to hold
her torch.

They drove in to support my wife

They drove in to support my wife who just
became,
a number, one of the Great Recession numbers,
one of the recently unemployed except this time
the number has a face, and the face has parents,
and a husband, and sisters, and in-laws,
and for a few days at our home at the beach
her family gathered around
and gathered her up
in their sweet arms,
we sleep late, have breakfast, read the paper,
write, dream,
do crossword puzzles, listen to Tony Bennett,
watch old movies,
lunch, nap, walk, walk sometimes, maybe, if,
and after supper
watching the movie "Ball of Fire"
with Gary Cooper, and Barbara Stanwyck,
the men go to bed first yawning and stretching,
the first one stumbles off around eight,
the next at eight-thirty, and God help me it was
late,
I went shuffling to bed at nine o'clock,
followed by everyone, and I mean everyone,

the whole tent folded up,
the loving arms of Jesus,
everything was in bed by ten.

Menopause, living with someone

Like a blunt hammer,
pounding the daylights,
out of,
anything that annoys,
anything that restricts,
directs, exchanges, moves, breathes,
breath is not a requirement,
where can I hide,
if only I,
had the awareness of one,
who was being stalked,
I could mount a defense,
somewhere, something, somehow.
I could slip under a door as a mouse,
a wondrously simple, beautiful,
life-affirming beeline,
to a safe place,
except for the rug,
the one being pulled,
that I didn't know,
I was standing on,
my legs twist,
and push the air,
trying to maintain,
balance,
God will not hide you.

I took the picture of my wife and her aged father

I took the picture of my wife and her aged father,
her arms around him,
this sweetest of moments.
and he seemed to just sit there,
flush with the comfort
of being held by his daughter,
and the daughter
flush with the moment
of being able to hold her father,
each suspended
in the affirmation
of the other,
and just for a moment,
a comma really,
this picture from,
humanity's story,
of the beauty, and struggle, and grace
of the continuity of this life,
and the people who pass through with us,
when it is our time to be held.

My father's song

It is said you are born into the perfect family
to teach God's lessons from where you are at
to bring you closer to God—
I was born into that perfect family
I had the perfect father
I have the perfect mother
I have perfect brothers
All my sisters are perfect
My wife is perfect
My children are perfect
I was born in the perfect town at the perfect time
I affirm all who bring me closer to God
I affirm the here and now
I affirm my becoming
I stand and sing
I will not be silent
I hold to each moment
I sing the passing of part of who I am
I sing the passing of part of who we are
I sing for the passing of the man
I sing for the passing of my father
I sing for the husband, the boss,

the provider, the protector,
the son, the brother, the soldier,
the keeper of the flame now passed,
for the time now gone,
for the time that we had,
for the memories of this life,
for the things that make us unique,
for the bluntness of his words,
for the sharpness of his wit,
for his gifts of management,
for his compassion of the common man,
for the difference he made,
and for all that he was and will be
for his parents we pray in heaven,
for his children left behind,
for his one brother that is with you now,
for your sisters who grieve for a good brother,
for my dear mother who has been his companion
    all these years,
for the child of God that comes to you now,
for the expressions of his love,
I release you to know his grace,
I release you to understand his love,
I release you to the cycle of life

that is part of God's grace and blessing
that comes to us all
I embrace the will of God
I embrace the sacredness of life.
I embrace the divinity within us.
I hold to our unknowing
to the mystery
to our becoming
to the things that will be
I know your parents by what I saw in you.
My children will know you by what they see in
me.
I pass now and hold to your memory.
I walk behind your steps.
I go where you go.
I walk where you walk.
I hold to what you hold.
I know what you know.
I sing my father's song.
And I pass it on.
And I pass it on.

The day I washed bed linen at Mother's house

Mother was aged, and angry, and depressed,
and I had forgotten that the years of pain, and mishaps
leading up to her increasing dependence,
where a body plots and schemes and resists
doing what the body has always promised it will do,
what it has always done simply and gracefully all these years,
now the pot of coffee struggles to pour itself
into the cup she drank from yesterday,
is even more uncooperative today,
her body is breaking promises, and cannot be trusted,
the hand is not pouring the way it has always poured,
and even the doctor's competence is in question,
if he were a mechanic, and charged for brakes he could not fix,
he would be fired, a refund demanded, a little hell could be raised,
so when I came to her room to see why she
shuffled with her coffee and walker right
by me without speaking.

it was because she was insulted, and outdone.
and I thought I could explain about the bed
    sheets I had washed,
and the things she was able to do yesterday
that she is unable to do today,
but I couldn't explain,
by myself,
and the wife back in our room
listening to every word as Mother let me have it
was no help at all.

Mother's walk

Mother is eighty-five now,
tired, hurting,
her walk twisted
and for years she refused to even use a cane.
said people might think she was old,
she has told me stories of coming back
from the store so tired,
she had to leave the groceries in the car,
come in the house, take a nap,
then go out, and bring 'em in,
this was given out like a documentary,
no anger, no judgment,
just an account of a body
breaking down little by little,
moment by moment,
just as surprised as the rest of us,
and the report today is:
she makes it halfway to the car,
and this is as far as she can go,
so stands there a little,
pondering her predicament,

and notices

a magnolia blossom

by the walk,

and it is magnificent, and sweet,

the kind of sweet that reminds one

of spring, and promise, and renewal,

so breaks it off,

and calls it a day.

Mother losing her memories

What does it mean when you start to lose things,
misplacing things like your eye drops,
or forget where you put your frying pan,
the one you have not used in years,
you wake up, and everything is missing,
the heating pad that fell behind the bed,
the amber glass tea pitcher,
the one you kept below the kitchen counter,
behind all the things you used to use when you
were young,
and our family was young,
and you were our unbroken link
to the future,
providing for us
as we are providing for ours,
doing what you were born to do
what we needed you to do,
and this time, in this moment,
you are trying to grab the memory of a tea
pitcher,
the one that holds the memories of a family
that pour from it strong, and sweet,
this season that was our becoming,

of our hope, and dreams,
and of our children
who will be,
who became
our own families
scattered across this country
who grew from this place beside you.

We who are lilies of the field

Mother fought like hell to stay alive yesterday,
and I struggled to let her go,
the right to die a natural death,
I never could get past the title of that document,
and all the family was there,
she was going to make it,
today was not the day,
but her time was close,
we all knew it, but no one could speak of it,
the withering months leading up to where we
    were,
so my brother and sister came from Florida,
some of the grandchildren,
and things were discussed,
and we stood there
wrapped in memories,
as leaves falling before winter,
piling up around our feet.

Mama I remember

Mama I remember going to your mother's house
    in Far City,
it was really called Forest City I realized later,
and then I saw that my very language,
the nuance of my speech,
its cadence,
its history,
this richness,
this river of culture,
each note,
each sound,
I realized I speak like you speak,
and I remember your mother,
Grandma lived in Far City in a mountain cabin
beside the road into town,
and that cabin rambled one room to the next,
and it rambled neat as a pin and glorious
full of memories and mountain things—
straw dolls, plates of china, trucker hats,
each pinned to the wall,
each memory,

a decoration,

a statement,

of a time and a place,

an attitude,

those little cedar boxes with the bark still on 'em,
or a weather rock that says, "If it's wet, it's
raining,"
I remember the excitement and hugs of those
visits,
I remember morning coffee around a red-
checkered tablecloth,
and I remember one time,
when we came to visit after dark unannounced
Grandma greeted us with a pistol.
and I remember no more visits after dark
unannounced.
I remember our lives unfolding
full of wonder and mystery and innocence,
Mom and apple pie,
Christmas, and Thanksgiving,
tradition,
family,

you are its heart—
you are the center from which we move,
and the place that we move to,
I remember the beach, coaster rides, cotton candy,
and picnics from the trunk of an old Ford,
I remember mountain trips to Maggie Valley,
    Ghost Town,
and Tweetsie Railroad and gunfights and Indian
    attacks
and Fred Kirby The Singing Cowboy.
I remember cable cars up the side of a slow
    mountain,
and ice cream floats in cola.
the family by cascading waterfalls framed in a
    picture,
all skinny and proud.
we did not know how good we were.
how perfect we were.
how beautiful we were.
it was our time.
I remember the Great Pee Dee River
speeding around in the boat Dad made—
we were the world and it was lightening.

how we loved to eat fresh panned-fried fish,
fries,
and hushpuppies by the bushel.
I remember bamboo poles, tackle, and cattails
along a mill pond's edge, said you saw me
swimming in the pond with the other mill
boys naked and I cried and said I would not
do it again,
straw forts angry bees old jars cardboard boxes
grassy hills.
played Kick the Can in the dark,
and when I was tired came home to you
who tucked me into bed.

Now I lay me down to sleep.
I pray the Lord my soul to keep.

Mama—you are a part of who I am,
and that part is sacred and precious
like mountain laurel in spring
or orchids beside a secret path
of red earth and green fields
I am the too-green corn

you are the rain
you are the framer
and I am the frame
you offer all that you have
and I, I am the greedy one
I take all that you give
know all who meet me,
meet a part of you
and in this Great Mystery—
we are your song,
and our song is real and without pretense.
our song—of which I am so proud.
our song—all southern and grit.
and we take our grits on a plate,
and our soup in a bowl
our eggs fried, our chicken fried,
our okra, squash, cornbread, ham, beef,
pork, fish, and iced tea,
our tea is strong enough to stand a spoon
and sweet
boiled in a pot.
I would carry the tea leaves out to put around
the red tip

on the corner of our house at the mill village,
and it grew to be glorious.
we were all glorious in your eyes.
let no one say a hurtful word about your children.
you would not have it.
so I was perfect.
unadorned to be who I was.
and I always needed you for the reminding,
for I sat on your couch without a word,
for not a word was needed.
Mama, help me remember who I am
and it was so easy for you.
I was always—your little boy.
I did nothing to receive your love.
and I knew I could do nothing more.
and I knew I could do nothing less.
I knew the ways of your silence.
the manner of your song,
always playing its melody for me.
forever soft and gentle and sweet
would bend me to its song.
you need not do anything.

there is nothing to prove.
nothing to do.
nothing left undone.
be who you are
because you are perfect.
like some invisible, gentle wind
that over the years gradually bends a tree
when no one is looking
I became a man and made my way
always returning,
always going to the well,
and you—always there,
and I—always your little boy.
Mama, I tell what you told me,
I give what you gave me.
I form my words as you wrote them to shape my
heart,
and I remember with each step of my form,
and each breath of my silence,
I remember our family,
and I remember how it is I,
who has had the privilege,
I have had this moment of family,

I am this nurtured seed,
I am part of something that is grand, and sacred,
and constant, and ever-flowing as are the seasons,
and from strength I speak,
from love I speak,
from just one,
who is in a line that comes from many,
I speak.
I speak from an ocean.
I speak from many brothers,
I speak from many sisters,
I speak from my children,
my children. my sisters. my brothers.
in this great, wonderful, sacred tapestry,
I grew tired, and came home to you
who tucked me into bed now I pray,
I pray for all those who showed us the way,
the ones before,
and the ones who come after,
as a child I pray,
I pray as a child,
by your side I pray.

Now, I lay me down to sleep.

I pray the Lord my soul to keep.

if I should die before I wake.

I pray the Lord my soul to take.

Mama you are a part of who I am,

and that part is sacred and precious

like mountain laurel in spring,

or orchids beside a secret path.

of red earth and green fields.

I am the too green corn.

you are the rain.

There is too much sun on too tender a place

There is too much sun on too tender a place
the first day back at work after Mother is gone,
and I have no reserve to handle the things that I
must do,
the whys, and hows,
the nuts and bolts,
the mechanics of doing what I do,
and oh how I have danced these long years taking on all
obstacles,
all problems, all things challenged, dashed,
solved
sometimes with only the softest nudge of
persuasion,
and sometimes commanding
the full weight of those from whose shoulders
I sprang—
this is my charge, this is who I am, oh beautiful
day,
but today
I take the steps,
but my feet are only pretending,
and even my lungs struggle to find air.

A time comes when both parents are gone

A time comes when both parents are gone,
and you are alone,
and there is no one to turn to,
no one left up ahead on the path
to show you the way.
you are the front line, oldest,
greeting mortality bare-teethed
just around the corner,
it is you who passes on the lessons,
it is you who shows the way,
it is you who lights the path
as the ones now gone
have shown you the way,
guardian of my father's guardian,
protector of our children's children,
my parents taught me
how to prepare the ground
marking each pit and tumble,
removing each pebble from my path,
I draw from them who protected me.
I draw from them who cheering
held me to this light.
I draw from them who

with all they held precious
cleared my path with petals and kisses,
I draw from my father,
I draw from my mother,
I, who was taught that
there are none more precious,
the one before you now,
who goes into this world.

When it's my turn

Give me strength
that when my body loses its integrity to take care
 of itself,
I will let go of this need to not depend on others,
help me Lord release me
from this last filament of expectation
I have of myself,
to hang on to what I was—
this saint, this sinner, this hero, this provider,
of things I have done
that I can no longer do,
give me strength to let go of parts I have played
singing songs I can no longer sing,
to love myself, and to those along the path
who held my hand,
who held me to this light,
to be gentle with this spot of fabric
when it's my turn.

The Angel of Maintenance

Of the angels of creation, I keep things working,
the bridges painted, bed rest, food,
ever notice how dirty and tired things get?
and how a little rain and a night's rest leave
    things,
ready for business,
I return things to zero, and from zero comes
gusto, surprise, strivings, leanings,
leanings that push and persuade
that stuff that you are
to become that stuff you were born to be,
you were meant to be,
to one's purpose,
why you are here.
I keep the field playable,
and I'm proud of my work,
thank the Angel of Maintenance,
not the other guy,
the Angel of Death,
the Angel of Death,
I am sick of all the press this guy gets,

oh, I'm so mysterious,
I would love to get this guy's head
between the door of an old Chevy
except I'd have to clean up the mess,
death and birth, death and birth,
that's all I ever hear,
how much skill do you have to have
to become the Angel of Death
when the truth is
that when I can't keep things going anymore
in comes the Angel of Death to take credit for
what I can't keep repaired,
the thing's old, or it's rusted,
the batteries corroded, a wire's broken,
and if the Angel of Death is bored and can't wait,
he runs it over with a truck,
drowns it in a lake,
where is the skill in that?
war, famine, disease.
I would love the Angel of Death to get off its butt
    one day,
and try to do my job.

My son in his thirties sometimes rides his mountain bike

My son in his thirties sometimes rides his
    mountain bike
sixty miles in a single day
and my daughter with her long legs
keeps in shape by kickboxing
they are crushing life and are perplexed
at why I seem to be slowing down
and struggling
so they teamed up in a Zoom meeting
to lecture me about my need to start
weight-bearing exercises
because if I don't
in ten years
I'll be feeble and if I am
it won't be out of ignorance
so I am working my way through the gym
fighting off decrepitude and I'll admit
their intervention surprised me
time moves softly for them
but occasionally

even they get a wakeup call

I saw the shock on my son's face
as he recounted a story
it was a story of transformation
a shift
in how he saw himself
and how someone of a
different generation saw him
it was a story of how he rode his bike
too close to a teenager on the trail
and the kid yelled
you old bitch.

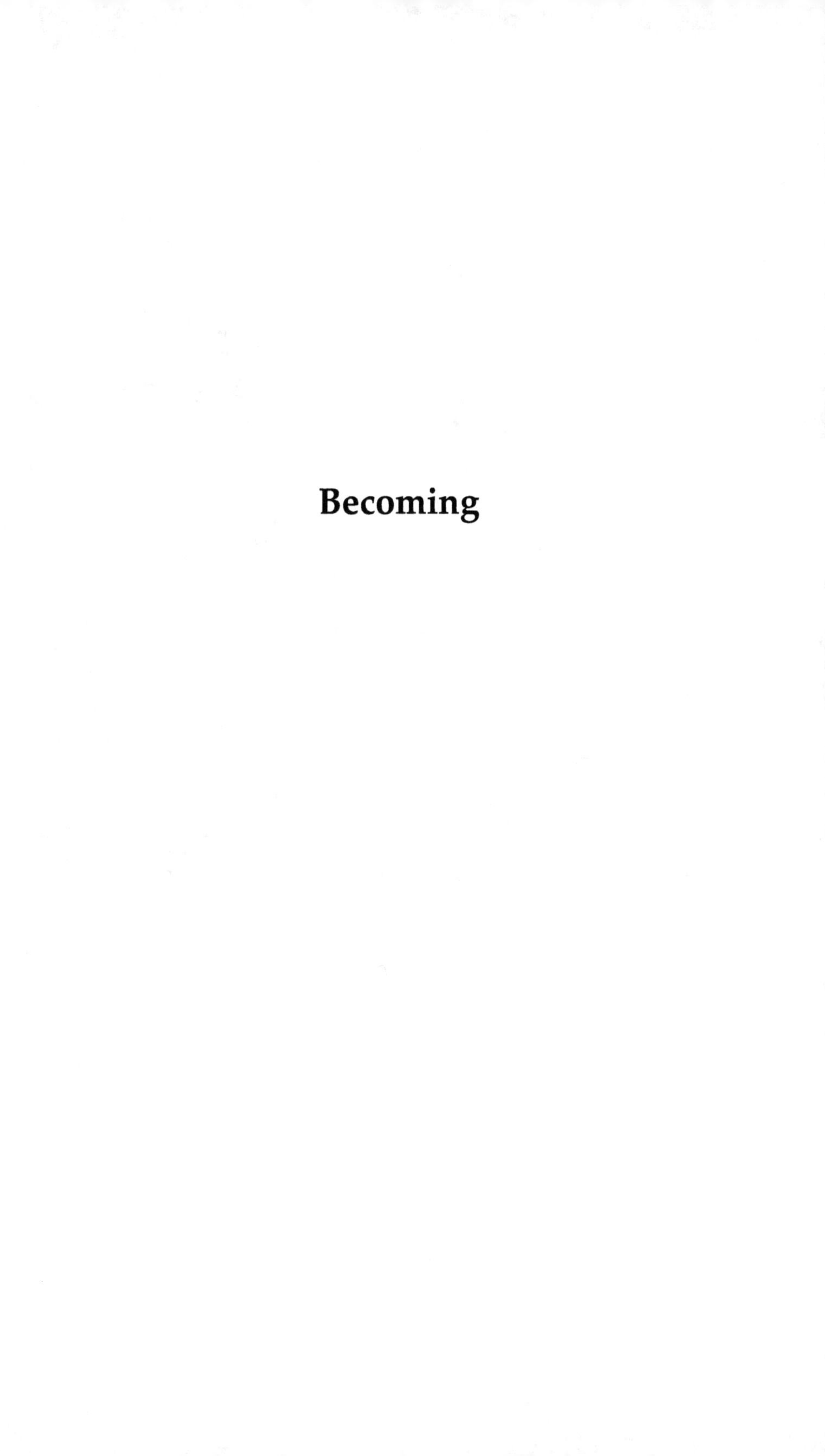

Becoming

Boot camp at the salt marsh

Lean to the front and let your arms fall,
loosely, listen, and learn.
be a frog.
now breathe the marsh.
hold its bouquet
pull it in.
what do you want?
is it damp?
make it dry.
is it sweet?
make it a Merlot.
and don't open your mouth when you breathe,
but focus on the gullet.
put your hips to it.
don't bead straight on.
keep the eyes left, then right.
look side to side like it's dangerous.
pull your mouth tight and smile.
you got one night.
take one breath.
divide the lows.
keep it green.

say—bul ya womp.
but only one syllable.
push the ends—let the ocean blow it.
bend the cattails.
wiggle your toes
now don't move a hair.
but sway and bend, wiggle 'em, get crazy,
do the dance like you love green,
but don't move except the eyes left, then right,
now while they're moving turn to the sweet spot.
visualize a schooner's mast.
to the wind.
all sails set.
canvas tight.
hold 'em steady, perfectly, perfectly
do not miss a whisper of air
that will keep those gullets taut.
now resonate,
and as you expand out keep on breathing in,
    then out,
get bug-eyed like you love green and skinny-
    legged frogs.
feel the wind shift and the trees sway.
bring the stars in,

whisper through the skin,
roll the eyes.
vibrate the teeth.
build a cathedral.
give it a sound.
make it sweat.
make it swell from the inside.
pull the muck side outside.
find your place.
call its name.
stretch the oceans.
shrink the tides.
be its song.
be the air.
be the dragonfly.
be your own nature.
who are you now?
be a frog.

And under this paint

You are crossing
Monet's Japanese Foot Bridge
and all the smiles
you think you would have
if all the wishes you have had
wait on the other side
and the memories
you wish you didn't
can't cross the bridge

And under this paint
you will find southern style fried chicken
in a blackened seasoned skillet
cornbread black-eyed peas
with Mama fixing biscuits
settings change
as your palette dreams

And under this paint
there is no mortgage
your kids are through college
and visit as their children

who are healthy and never age
the house is always clean
things go back
to where they belong
every room has a view
to a garden

And under this paint
your wife smiles
and brings you tea
says you're the king
and you are
of a small country
who are pleased
you are king

And under this paint
you are an artist
a philosopher
a scientist
a priest
a lover
a dreamer
and you find everyone

all kings and queens
all lovers
all dreamers
all shades and colors
all lush
all broad
and bold
lolling
where contentment floats
like a lily
on the water
as moments of color
not measured in time
God speaks
and as a friend
withholds no privileges
holds no secrets
no powers
no apologies
no regrets
and you cross Monet's bridge
and dream as paint dreams

Meditation

I go to my World War I vintage craft
button the straps of my helmet
zip up my leather jacket and tighten the goggles
the double wings held by wire slowly at first
down the runway
the lessons begin to pick up speed
the hidden agendas begin to sputter and smoke
a few guide cables pop like piano wire
the wheels bounce a couple of times
and I begin to move into myself
proud of my insignia
proud of who I am and proud that I am proud
I think of the squadron I am from and our motto
    Die Hard
the thoughts come like a dog fight as flak comes
    from my gun
I mow them down and watch as they burst into
    flames.
where did I put my library card
the librarian said they will ask for it my next visit
and I only had six visits a year without it

and that was one—rat tat tat
the upcoming wedding
my children in their first jobs
the barking dog that kept me up last night
I am behind that one now lining it in my sights
    just up ahead of me
no it's the electric company marking our front
    yard for digging
the thoughts come freely now
and I am not flying in my backyard
my guide wires no longer work
I can't remember my motto
I forgot my insignia
and that I am proud
and God help me
I'm in a barrel roll

In meditation

In meditation
I close my eyes
carried on a sound
until I become—
this breath,
this feeling,
this silence.
silence that is vast,
formless,
still.
stillness that speaks:
there is no place I need go,
there is no place I am more,
there is no place I am less.
I am the sun.
the spiraling swirl of dust.
the turn of seasons.
the watch spring.
the roof of the universe.
I am its floor.
the endless place.
its point.
the sacred expression.

The practice of meditation

It's a journey of expansion
some language
a thought
a word
and when you are close to infinity
there is sweetness at its edge
consciousness that just is
no yesterdays
nothing tomorrow
no appointments to keep
none missed
you can't speak it
because the words have yet to form
the experience is unfolding
on the level of feeling
and it's about expansion
and it's about boundaries
and it's about silence
and it's about you
and me
and God
and perfect pirouettes
it's about dancing

I hold on to my prayers

I hold on to my prayers
I start at the level of speech
floating and expanding
I go below words
I go below the intellect
below ego
and without words
I remember
I know this prayer
I have used
all these years
and when I am here
all I need is the feeling
of your presence.

Prayer for change

Lord forgive me
for what I said when I was hungry
and all the things I've said after eating a good
meal
and when eating bad food
and between meals
and when I've eaten too much
Lord forgive me for measuring my sins around food
because I was made in thy image
and you must love potato chips, ice cream, and
chocolate
forgive me when I go to Costco knowing
that when I buy a pillowcase full of potato chips
I'll eat the whole bag in three days
and blame my wife for not stopping me
forgive me for what I say when my wife makes
me mad
she knew before she married me that I say things
I shouldn't say
when the facts sometimes interfere with how I
thought the world was
and what I say in private

when I think no one is listening
and all the gleeful mean-spirited words
that come out of my mouth
jubilantly celebrating all the times
my fellow traveler on the path
tripped over their own shoestrings
and all the hard words I've said in public
when someone honks at me
for driving too slow in the left passing lane
I was going slow that's true
but I thought the speed limit applied to both
lanes
and for all the times I have pulled in front of
someone
who should have seen me
and for taking more than my fair share of…
forgive me if I can't think of anything
and Lord help all the people I see
doing and saying foolish things
to accept responsibility
for things
they might need changing

Amen

Wile E. Coyote

Somewhere in the Southwest
Monument Valley maybe
dotted in mesas and buttes
the Acme Corporation can provide
whatever your imagination
can come up with
by mail order
which I thought was
very convenient
a Dehydrated Boulder
Batman Outfit
Rocket Sled
Jet Powered Roller Skates
Earthquake Pills
but nothing worked
as it should
and the coyote
goes up like a match
is squashed flat
or falls to the bottom
of a canyon

(this took a while)
which I found
very pleasing
and I especially
got comfort from knowing
there's just one rule
the coyote will always go hungry
and the way the laws of physics
are suspended and applied
so unfairly
is particularly satisfying
the Wile E. Coyote
would chase the Road Runner
right off a cliff and stand on air
and I'm right there with him
breaking the laws of physics
but as any fool knows
when you realize
you're doing the impossible
that's when you're coming down.

To the people I hear changing gears from my living room in Lenoir

What the world sees
and what you think you are presenting
is not what you think it is
when I hear your gears announcing themselves
struggling and winding
slipping between their metal teeth
amplified by your modified tailpipes
I imagine a Neanderthal
with their sloping brow and knuckles
dragging the ground
getting up each morning late for work
when I hear you change gears from my living
room
I wonder what part of you is missing
by your need to announce yourself
through your tailpipe
I want to help you look
the whole world wants to help you look
a mother's love
to be held and cuddled and told again and again

I hear you
I am so sorry the world didn't notice you
    standing there
I think you are just wonderful the way you are
there is no need to puff yourself up to
    compensate
let me help you find what you are missing
you broken-winged butterfly
you lost adorable kitten
let me help you put yourself together again
you forty-five-piece porcelain set of chipped
    china

My students take the end of grade test during a tropical storm

It was a bushes whacking glass
kind of rain, the kind of rain
that a stack of frogs might sing
"We Are the Champions"
arms locked cheek to cheek
it don't get any better
than this blustery kind of rain,
and I love the word blustery,
it's a Pooh Hundred Acre Wood word
to describe weather
that is terrible, and frightening,
but not so frightening as to think
one would come to harm,
but just frightening enough
to have an adventure,
my students hunkered down
as this year is
distilled, inhaled,
washed down, quaffed,
measured, sorted,
our whistle wet
into this spud of a test

our Opus Dei,
our capstone,
our ne plus ultra
my fifth-grade students,
and I amidst this
magnificent background
of a storm
loosed their knowledge
rising from the sea like a Kraken.

Living requires preparation

I have never been busier
I even get up at five just so I can get to it
but before I start the important stuff of my life
before I begin to live
the reason why stars were born and died
exploding their guts all over creation
to give me the building blocks necessary
to do the important stuff I was born to do
I cram in a little doomscrolling
because I want to know what happened while I
    slept
I saw this meme that captured my situation
"Ninety percent of people who doomscroll quit
right before they find something really
    interesting"
Facebook,
Quora,
the news
then a random digest of articles based on my
    interests
I greedily roll over the titles till one catches my

eye
"How to prevent a stroke"
I dive in sweaty like a crack addict
how do I prevent this horror
it says, "Don't smoke."
I'm a sucker for best towns list
did I do all right moving here
a recipe for chocolate cake with thin layers
something the Cat in the Hat would carry on a
white plate while riding a unicycle about to
ruin Christmas
I save this one to a folder marked recipes
that someday I will make

And God created heaven on earth

To ensure conditions for success
God decided to make all of humanity
ninety-nine point nine percent
from the same genetic stuff
so people could see
that all people
are brothers and sisters
from the same family
and so things would be
peachy rosy
and we'd love one another
like brothers and sisters
and we'd work and play together
like champs
but that one tenth
of one percent
difference
upset a lot of people
and God had to stay up late
and work weekends

My sister is living the life of a Kellogg's cereal box cover

My sister is living the life
of a Kellogg's cereal box cover,
she wakes up yawns opens her
sweet hard-working eyes
to the tallest greenest field of corn
this side of paradise,
and there is a backdrop
of a radiating sun,
and it goes cover to cover,
Conestoga wagons,
trail masters,
Olympic athletes,
and the Colonel John Wayne
rallying his troops,
it's a morning sun,
with an old farmhouse, barns, sheds,
and not just any kind of shed,
it's the one with a mile high roof
where eagles rest, and tractors plow
whatever is wholesome,

and good, and green,
and it's always never planted on
anything less than forty acres,
and on this cereal box
there is one of them perky roosters
that greets you, and the world
to get up, and get going
and without saying a word
speaks of morning goodness
except this is a mean rooster,
and just so happens on this cereal box,
my sister is tall, and beautiful, and athletic,
and when life comes at her,
she is packing a cast iron frying pan.

If I were in charge, I could do better

I go about this life
plodding along a path seemingly of pure chance
the people I meet
the places I live
the lessons I learn
one moment I am the teacher
grinding into my fellow traveler
the lesson they need
and then on the turn of a dime
I am the student
the fracas tied up with string lands on my desk
chaos, floods, wrong turns, chance encounters
I'd have none of this flying by the seat of your
    pants business
if I were in charge, I could do better
there would be an agenda, an outline,
each lesson would follow a syllabus
announced in advance hard copies going home
having us born with a propensity for
    uncontrollable desires
for worldly intoxicating indulgences

is like dumping a load of sand
between the monkey bars and swing set
on the kindergarten playground and posting a
    sign
"Children: Do not play in the sand."
we all jump in, and feel terrible about it
and that's not fair,
is it?
I would provide no temptation a student could
    not handle
and the student wouldn't have to figure out
what it is they're supposed to learn
because everybody would know what the rules are
    up front
"This is God.
Nothing happens by chance.
You get what you earn, and the lessons follow
    you
from school to school. Do your best."
and dadgummit!
when they've mastered what is taught
they'd get a passing grade, a diploma
a star, something that would tell them

where they stood
stamped right on their paper
or pinned to their shirt
would be a note
"Johnny got a star today in greed.
Had two pencils. Gave Jimmy one.
He's making progress."
and to create conditions for success
each student would be taught on their
    instructional level
I wouldn't put a drunk in charge of an oil tanker
and turn him loose on Prince William Sound
the lessons would be spiral in nature
building on previous material
I would ensure everybody had been fed and
    rested
before the lessons began
the classrooms would be well lit
comfortable seating
free breakfast
and I wouldn't try to do the whole thing in six
    days,
I'd take my time!

forbidden apples?
there'd be no baiting with apples
apples would be welcome in my classroom
and appreciated especially
if your grades were short
apples would be helpful
if I were in charge.

Do you love me?

At this point in Dad's story it's late
both legs gone to diabetes mini strokes cataracts
this six-foot-two World War II veteran who
climbed poles hanging wire dodging mortars
running up mountains in Europe
is now rolling his wheelchair
through the house with nothing to do
but supervise Mother
and she doesn't like it
says everything about him
is broke
except his mouth
they are both exasperated
they have plots side by side
and she wants to be buried
with her back to him
and Dad
Dad says he doesn't even think
Mother wants him to come out of his bedroom—
thought she was scared some woman might see him
I miss them and just the act of remembering

I feel fuller and now
my daughter my son their children
and our words and what we do together
is turning into our own season
and in each word
at each turn
at this point in my own story
it's later than I like to think
and I have come to realize
that we make our own history
and just now my wife
is leaving bags and boxes
about the floor for the cat to play with—
says its enrichment
and when I stomped them
going out the door
I meant to say
what my parents meant to say
that we are angels
looking for our wings
and with each word
with each step I take
what I mean to say is

I love you so much
will you let me in
can my heart
be part of your heart
do you love me?

First steps

You hold to furniture to cross a room unaware
how thick the carpet is beneath you
how soft the chairs are around you
and how everywhere there are hands
ready to pick you up and hold
and embrace and point to places
familiar places
you can sense from your child
I call to you now from that place
how you held a favorite doll
or rode a forgotten horse
how you did it perfectly
your play was perfect
your imagination was perfect
the way the doll lay in your arms
the horse by your side
the way of your silence unadorned
you did not know how perfect you were
now remember how you move across this room
without thought or regret or effort or hesitation
you proclaimed with every step and word

with your silence and your walk
with the flow of your hair
and the turn of your form
I am here now free
and all people
in all places will applaud
and my heart will be a garden
and your words the rain.

If I knew what I know now

If I knew what I know now
I would have been seventy years old when I was
born
I would have known to do as a child does
to love as a child loves
I would have known
to find joy in a jar of bees
to collect lightning bugs
and butterflies, and frogs
and I would have known
when to let them go
to crack open rocks
rocks that astonish
and take my breath
to pass time singing
to doodle bugs
with twigs in the dirt
and that a cardboard box
will carry me down a grassy hill
I would know that four-leaf clovers
are hard to find and water in any pond

will carry a rock if you hit it just right
how to make forts out of straw
and I would have known
while building a fort
that I was just building a fort
not how long it will stand
or if it will be there tomorrow
and when in that moment
it is the only moment I have
and tomorrow will come
and yesterday is already gone.

In Hong Kong

In Hong Kong we had
pan-fried fish for breakfast,
I had never had fish for breakfast before,
never put the two together,
I sometimes eat breakfast for supper
eggs, toast, home fries, grits,
and get this rush out of doing
what you wouldn't normally expect,
I surprise myself
in the unexpected routine of things,
even if it is only by eating the same things
at times I don't normally eat them,
I am pleased with how original I have become,
and even as I am unfolding,
at each well documented stage of life,
I am surprised when I get there,
sucker-punched by it all,
in childlike awe I go,
into this mysterious sacred search of
the very humanity that is so easy to recognize
in everyone, and everything except myself

not recognizing that this beauty I see in others,
they see in me,
and I remember how I walk
like spiral cones of incense might walk,
burning from the ceiling
of a temple.

Everybody is speaking

The stop sign is demanding, the blinking lights,
the wood of the tree, and the trees that are made
    stalk like,
buildings of sky, upward rising cities, the we
    who are talking,
speaking, from rusty metal, and lighted signs,
and from the intersections,
I can hear it in the chinks of our armor,
in the dying of our coral,
in our sonnets,
and in our yearnings,
I can hear it in our sun,
our lyrical rising,
and in the spiraling of our skies,
in the ruminations of gods,
and in the power of thunder,
and in the fullness of our moon,
I can hear it ripple in the water,
in the trails of bent grass,
I can hear how we are
speaking, speaking, speaking,

in the river over its bank,
how we are
seeking, seeking, seeking,
in this rich loam of land,
in the foam of our seas,
and in the affirmation of the tides,
and in the tides, and in the tides, and in the tides
they said, she said,
and in our hymns
I can hear it singing, singing, singing,
we hear, I hear, she is, they are. I am.
we hear, I hear, she is, they are. I am.
he said, and there was light, and she said,
do you like apples, and I said, and he said,
everybody is speaking,
everybody is trying.
everyone
O my soul.

Sometimes I dream in watercolor

Sometimes I dream in watercolor
the pigments are still wet
the memories are still fresh
for paint knows where it must go
it knows what it must do
it must find the tender spots
the uneven surface
and I dream and dream
and all the time it picks up speed
the strokes are more certain
the lines take on definition
until it is set into place
and I began to see
those things I need to see
those feelings I hold
those things I need to understand
those hidden parts of myself
beautifully formed and delicate
as a bouquet of flowers

The long walk

I start out for a walk
and walk and walk and walk
to a bookstore for tea
about four miles
coming back at night
with a flashlight strapped to my belt
dangling light about the pavement
block by block
step by step
I notice the life of Park Avenue
always littered with old couches
and mattresses and discarded TVs
for pick up because somebody
has been evicted or moved
it is a snapshot of the comings and goings
of the people whose lives I intersect
as I move along this shared path
that runs in front of the houses
and as I move I notice
how planted my feet are
with each step the feeling that

there is nothing I need
but my feet and this pavement
there is nothing I need
but this grass
this weed
this sound
that grows around the banks
of this road
this forest of stars and trees
and this path I am on
there is nothing I need
to cross step by step
between the flow of cars
onto the next street
down the next block
the next turn
there is nothing I need
this pavement
this night.

To a teacher at the Juvenile Evaluation Center, Swannanoa, North Carolina

This is written loudly for a teacher
because they come so quietly to you
as wards of the state and leave without a trace
I see your handwriting on their lives
I have read their daily paragraphs
and seen them struggle
with writings humorous, vulgar, and angry
with needs so great only your approval will do
or for love show them where the boundaries are
so you go
from student to student
from year to year
and they are hurt
if you are not planted by their side
and for those who fumble
over elementary words known to most
those big pretenders who pretend not to care
and at the same time go to extraordinary lengths
to vie secretly for your attention
and for those who carefully hide

fearful, their starving eyes
and it is those eyes that tell the lesson—
never loosen a tight gut
for it deflects injury and neglect
and an expectation withdrawn
is one you never have to meet
and over time has no memory of its birth
so in the end you are all they've got,
for God places understanding
where it is needed the most,
for you are there
and you are there regardless
of what happens around you.
like the seasons from which
branches bud, and push out new leaves
that are expressions of the sun
brilliant as the colors of fall
the stillness of winter
the birth of spring
the fullness of summer,
you are the seasons
that flow into the other
never ending, ceaseless

as the years mature as decades

and as a force of nature

for those who could not be

there for them—

I see your acceptance in their eyes.

This journey we are on

Do not allow what you have to do
for a living define you.
separating that which you are
into that which you are not,
this feeling of not belonging,
this quality of unwantedness,
the rain,
the diminished part of ourselves,
those times when we are struggling,
and this awkward uncertainty
of how things really are—
not what we expected,
and the realization that
we do not know as much
as we thought we did,
and the questions about
the eggshell,
about our fragility,
and all this spinning,
and how busy we are
rushing to places,

important places,
time-sensitive places,
of questions
about our seeming, random
place in things,
and the things
we think we should be,
what we could be,
that have not delivered as promised,
and those moments
when we are so close knowing
who we really are we can taste it.
this journey of our perfection,
of our becoming,
and of our sun,
and the rain,
judging ourselves,
and everyone,
and everything
and everybody,
even God,
and how perfect
it all is.

Birthdays pass

Birthdays pass
I get married
my children grow up and leave
and one day they call
letting me know
grandchildren are near
and I remember
how I used to be so shy
and unsure of myself
my world
my path
was not that special
so I went about this life
from place to place
as a tourist
but looking back now
I see
how lit up under the passing moons
and stars, and tides and I
I have walked this path
I was meant to walk

doing the things
I was meant to do
and things are unfolding
as they are meant to unfold
it was a path gilded in gold
and lit up in neon

Becoming part of the seasons

Babies buds beginnings
everything begins with spring
and everything begins
with zeal
and wonderment
and joy
just to be here
and I have been around for many such wonders
watching life renew itself
and I remember time
turning into family
children
a spouse who loves me
and a job where people
desperately need what I have to offer
my purpose drove
the summer of my life
the arc of my trajectory
the why of my spring
where everything was clear
for why I am here

and then it became

the end of summer

then fall

and now the beginning of winter

my life built from all the springs

and all the summers

and all the falls

of all the plantings before me

now this rich loam

You there, reading this poem

I,

the consciousness

that I am,

eternal,

indestructible,

the consciousness,

that cannot be burned,

or cut, or marked, or wet,

the consciousness that can travel

at the speed of thought,

the consciousness that is already there,

the consciousness that says:

there is no time, or space, or limitation,

the consciousness that experiences

itself,

unfolding

unto itself,

by itself,

for itself,

you there,

reading this poem,

you are the very one I address,
saying:
I see a light.
and by light
I mean you,
the universe,
the sacred expression,
and you see me,
and we dance,
and we move,
into the other,
and we dance,
and we move,
into the other,
and we dance,
and we move,
into the other.

Acknowledgments

I wish to acknowledge the helpers of my life. First, thanks to all the storytellers. Growing up on a cotton mill village, I gathered many a night with the men and boys who listened to Charles "Redeye" Diggs as he weaved his stories. Thanks to the thousand Redeye Diggses I have met growing up in the South, who continue to inspire me. I recognize Bill Matthews for fully seeing me, and whispering in my ear, "No one knows what you might do one day." I acknowledge Professor Maurice Martinez, University of North Carolina at Wilmington, for sponsoring the UNC-W Poetry Slam, my first public reading. After writing for fifteen years reading only to my wife, this was the first time I thought of myself as a poet. I am grateful for the help of Scott Owens for taking me aside and affirming me. It is his encouragement and assistance that has led me to publish this work with Redhawk. Finally, I am thankful for Julie Martin, my editor, wife, mentor, muse, and dearest friend anyone can have on this earth. She has encouraged me from my first line to my last.

About the Author

R. Steve Martin was born in 1952 in Wadesboro, North Carolina, into a family of cotton mill workers. He spent his childhood in the mill village. He holds degrees from East Carolina University and Francis Marion University. He taught public school, managed a facility for the developmentally disabled, and taught at a juvenile prison. He began writing poetry at age forty. He lives in Lenoir, North Carolina, with his wife. They have two children and two grandchildren.

www.ingramcontent.com/pod-product-compliance
Lightning Source LLC
LaVergne TN
LVHW050645100826
845148LV00011B/1986

* 9 7 9 8 8 9 9 3 3 0 2 0 9 *